Somewhere Safe

by Emily Drage

Cover design and interior layout by Emily Drage.
ISBN: 978-1-7642182-0-7
First edition.

Dedication

To all my wonderful foster children,

Who have grown to be amazing humans.

Your courage, your kindness, and your resilience inspire
me every day.

This story is for you!

Table of Contents

Author's Note ....
Acknowledgements ....

Part 1: Breaking
Chapter 1: The Explosion ....
Chapter 2: The Mask ....
Chapter 3: Cracks ....

Part 2: Cracks in the Wall
Chapter 4: The Wall ....
Chapter 5: The Quiet Room ....
Chapter 6: Triggers ....

Part 3: Healing
Chapter 7: The Breakthrough ....
Chapter 8: Small Steps ....
Chapter 9: The Key ....

Epilogue: Somewhere Safe ....

Author's Note

When I first sat down to write this story, I thought about all the incredible young people I've had the privilege to know—children who have lived through more pain, upheaval, and uncertainty than anyone ever should, yet who somehow still find a way to hope, to dream, and to keep going.

This book is for you.

I know foster care can feel lonely. I know it can feel like nobody really sees you, like nobody understands what it's like to pack your life into a bag over and over again and try to start fresh. I know how hard it is to let yourself trust, to let yourself believe that you deserve good things.

But you do.

You deserve safety.
You deserve kindness.
You deserve love.
You deserve the chance to build a life that feels like your own.
You deserve your quiet place!

I hope this story reminded you that you are not alone—and that your story is far from over. Every step you take, no matter how small, is worth celebrating.

To all my wonderful foster children—past, present, and future—you inspire me every single day. You've
grown into such amazing, strong, beautiful humans, and I am so proud of you.

With love,
Emily Drage

Acknowledgements

This book was written for the kids who never felt like they had a place to belong.

You are seen.
You are valued.
You are worthy of love.

To the countless young people who grow up in foster care, who carry more than their share of pain yet still dare to dream—your strength is breathtaking.

To the foster parents, social workers, and mentors who show up day after day: thank you for proving that kindness matters.

To my friends and family, who listened to every draft and cheered me on when I felt like giving up—your faith in me gave me wings.

And finally, to every reader who picks up this book and sees themselves in Jaden's story: you're not alone.

Part 1: Breaking

Chapter 1: The Explosion

Jaden kept his hood up the entire car ride, even though the summer heat pressed in through the rolled-down window, baking his legs against th cracked vinyl seat. A bead of sweat trickled down his back, but he didn't care. The hoodie was like armour — heavy, stifling, but safe.

He sat slumped in the corner of the back seat, duffel bag at his feet, his sneakers scuffed from kicking gravel in yet another parking lot that morning. Outside the window, neighbourhoods drifted past — green lawns, white fences, families unloading groceries. He didn't bother looking too closely.

It didn't matter what the house looked like. They never did.

Ms. Hines, his social worker, kept glancing at him in the rear-view mirror. She'd open her mouth every now and then, like she was about to say something, then close it again and sigh.

That was fine. He didn't want her to talk. He didn't want to hear another speech about how "this one's different" or "this could really work if you just try."

He was done trying.

The car slowed as they turned down a quiet street lined with maples, their leaves glowing golden in the late afternoon light. She pulled up in front of a little yellow house, the kind with peeling paint and flower pots on the steps. Two bikes leaned against the porch rail.

Ms. Hines shifted into park and turned in her seat. "Here we are," she said, her voice soft, like she was afraid of him breaking.

Jaden didn't move.

She watched him for a second, then said, "I know you've heard this before, Jaden. But the Ortegas... they're good people. They know about... your history. And they still said yes. That has to count for something, doesn't it?"

He didn't answer.

Her face softened. "Kiddo... just try. Please. For me?"

He tightened his arms over his chest and stared at the floorboards.

When she got out of the car, he followed, dragging his duffel bag by the broken handle.

The front door of the house opened before they even reached the porch.

A woman stood there, short and sturdy, her brown skin glowing in the sunlight. Her dark curls were pulled into a messy bun, and there was flour on her hands.

"You must be Jaden," she said, her voice calm and warm.

He didn't answer.

"That's okay," she said quickly, her smile unwavering. "You don't have to say anything yet. Why don't you come inside? Dinner's almost ready."

The smell of garlic and roasted chicken hit him as soon as he stepped through the door. He hated how his stomach growled.

The dining room table was set. A tall man — Mr. Ortega — rose to greet them, his expression kind but unreadable. At the table sat two kids: a little girl with bright braids who grinned at him like she already knew him, and a boy about his age who barely glanced up from his phone.

"This is Mr. Ortega. And these are our kids, Gabby and Luis," Mrs. Ortega said.

"Hi!" Gabby chirped, waving.

Luis grunted something that could've been "hey" without looking up.

Jaden kept his hood up and his eyes down.

While Mrs. Ortega and Ms. Hines whispered in the kitchen, Jaden stood awkwardly by the table, his fists in his hoodie pocket. He heard their words clearly:

"...aggression..."
"...emotional outbursts..."
"...needs structure..."

It made his stomach turn. He hated when they talked about him like he was just a file.

When Mrs. Ortega came back, she smiled at him again, like nothing was wrong. "Why don't you sit? You must be hungry."

He sat.

Didn't speak.

Didn't let himself hope.

Because if he stayed quiet, maybe they'd let him stay.

Maybe.

Chapter 2: The Mask

For the first week, Jaden put on the mask.

He woke early every morning, made his bed so tight you could bounce a quarter off it. He lined up his sneakers by the door, kept his hoodie folded on the chair, and said "yes ma'am" and "no sir" to every question.

Mrs. Ortega always smiled at him like she couldn't tell it was fake.

Gabby trailed him around like a shadow. "Wanna play Candyland?" she asked every single day, holding the box under her chin with her big hopeful eyes.

Every single day, he shook his head.

She'd pout for half a second, then skip away, already humming.

Luis mostly ignored him. Sometimes, though, Jaden caught him watching, like he was waiting for something to happen.

Every night, lying awake in bed staring at the ceiling, Jaden felt the weight in his chest grow heavier. The mask cracked a little more each day.

And finally, it shattered.

It happened over something stupid — just a normal Tuesday, after school.

Mrs. Ortega was making dinner when she handed him the trash bag. "Can you take this out for me?" she asked with a smile.

And everything inside him boiled over.

"I'm not your servant!" he shouted, his voice breaking.

Mrs. Ortega froze, still holding the bag.

"You think just because I live here you can boss me around?!"

The bag split open on the floor as she dropped it. Gabby gasped. Luis appeared in the doorway, his phone dangling at his side.

Mr. Ortega stood slowly, but didn't say a word.

Jaden's hands were shaking. His chest heaved.

He kicked the trash can so hard it rattled against the cabinets, then ran upstairs, two at a time, and slammed his door hard enough to make the frame groan.

He stood there, leaning on the door, his breath ragged. His face was hot, and he hated himself for it.

Through the floorboards, he thought he heard Mrs. Ortega say softly, "It's okay. He's just scared."

But he didn't feel scared.

He felt furious.

Chapter 3: Cracks

The next morning, Jaden stayed in bed, the hood of his sweatshirt pulled tight.

Gabby peeked in at one point, holding her Candyland box like a peace offering. When he didn't move, she left without a word.

Later, Luis passed by and muttered something about him "freaking out."

Around noon, there was a soft knock on his door.

"Jaden?"

No answer.

After a moment, the door creaked open a few inches. Mrs. Ortega didn't come in. Instead, she sat on the floor outside his room, her back against the wall.

"You know," she said after a long silence, "when Luis was your age, he put two holes in this wall."

Jaden didn't move.

"Right there," she continued, her voice light. "And there. Had to patch them both. He even broke his hand once. Emergency room and everything."

Something inside Jaden twisted. He buried his face in his pillow. "…That's dumb," he muttered.

She chuckled quietly. "It was. But you know what? I didn't love him any less. And I won't love you any less, either. Even if you're mad. Even if you kick trash cans or slam doors."

His throat tightened painfully.

"You don't even know me," he whispered.

"You're right," she said gently. "But I want to."

She stayed there for a while longer, just breathing, just being.

Before she left, she said softly, "I made grilled cheese if you get hungry."

When her footsteps faded, Jaden rolled onto his back and stared at the ceiling.

And for the first time in a long time, the weight in his chest felt just a little bit lighter.

Not much.

But enough to notice.

Part 2: Cracks in the Wall

Chapter 4: The Wall

The next few days passed in a strange sort of quiet.

Jaden came down for meals, muttering a stiff "thanks" whenever Mrs. Ortega set a plate in front of him, then retreating to his room as soon as he was done. He avoided everyone's eyes.

Luis avoided him now too, always slipping his headphones on the moment Jaden walked into a room. Gabby still followed him sometimes, though. She'd stand in the doorway to his room, her big brown eyes wide with a question she never quite asked out loud.

"Wanna play?" she said one afternoon, her voice soft.

Jaden shook his head, not even looking at her.

Her shoulders sagged, but she nodded and went back downstairs.

Safer this way.

It was easier to stay behind the wall.

One evening, almost a week after he'd exploded in the kitchen, Jaden was sitting on the back steps, his hood pulled low. The air was cool, and the faint scent of cut grass hung in the breeze. Across the street, neighbour kids raced up and down on bikes, their laughter shrill and bright.

He watched them without really seeing them.

Mrs. Ortega's footsteps were quiet as she came around the corner.

"Mind if I sit?" she asked.

Jaden shrugged.

She sat anyway, easing herself down beside him. They sat in silence for a while, listening to the whir of bike tires and the occasional bark of a dog down the block.

Finally, she said, "You know, I get mad too sometimes."

Jaden snorted softly. "Yeah, right."

Her lips quirked into a faint smile. "You think I don't?"

"You're… nice," he muttered. "Nice people don't get mad."

Her eyebrows rose. "That so?"

Jaden kept his eyes on his sneakers.

"When I was your age," she said, her voice gentle, "I used to throw things. Broke a whole set of plates once. My mom didn't know what to do with me. I was scared, but I didn't know how to say it. So it came out as mad."

Jaden risked a quick glance at her, her face soft in the fading light.

"You don't have to talk about it yet," she added. "But whenever you're ready… I'll listen."

For the first time, her words didn't make him bristle.

He stared down at the toes of his sneakers, scuffed and worn.

The wall stayed up.

But maybe — just maybe — a crack had formed.

Chapter 5: The Quiet Room

The next few days were better, and worse.

He kept his head down at school, ignored the kids who stared at him like he was something strange. But in math class, one of them snickered just loud enough for him to hear.

"Hey, don't go psycho on us, foster freak."

His hands clenched under the desk. His pulse roared in his ears.

By the time he got home, he was shaking with rage. He barely managed to get through the door before storming upstairs, slamming his bedroom door so hard the mirror rattled on the wall.

A few minutes later, there was a knock.

"Jaden?" Mrs. Ortega's voice was calm, even.

He didn't answer.

"Come with me," she said.

He wanted to tell her to leave him alone. But her voice was so steady, and he was so tired, that he followed anyway.

She led him to the end of the hall, to a door he'd never noticed before. She unlocked it and pushed it open.

"This," she said, "is the quiet room."

It wasn't really a room. More like a large walk-in closet. But it was warm and soft, lit by strings of fairy lights that cast a golden glow over beanbags and blankets piled neatly in a corner. Books lined a low shelf, puzzles stacked on top. The air smelled faintly of lavender.

Jaden stood in the doorway, suspicious. "…What is this?"

"It's a place to feel safe," she said simply.

He frowned deeper, but she only smiled.

"You can come here whenever you want," she added. "No one bothers you here. You don't have to talk. You just... be."

He hesitated, then stepped inside.

The floor was carpeted and soft. He sank down onto one of the beanbags, burying his hands in the kangaroo pocket of his hoodie.

Mrs. Ortega didn't follow him in. She just pulled the door halfway closed.

"Stay as long as you need," she said gently.

At first, he sat stiff and wary. But after a while, his shoulders loosened, and he stretched out on the beanbag, staring at the lights.

And then, without meaning to, he cried.

Quietly, into his sleeve, so no one would hear.

When he was done, he didn't feel weak.

He felt... lighter.

Chapter 6: Triggers

Things weren't perfect after that.

But they were better.

Jaden started using the quiet room when the anger in his chest got too sharp.
He'd sit on the beanbag and breathe until it dulled to something manageable.

Sometimes Mrs. Ortega would slip a snack through the door — an apple,
crackers, a cookie. Sometimes she sat outside and talked about nothing at all.

One night, she said, "We all have triggers, Jaden. Things that set us off. That's
not the problem. The problem is what we do with them."

He didn't answer. But he thought about her words as he fell asleep that night.

A few days later, at lunch, it happened.

The same boy — tall, loud, with a smirk that made Jaden's fists itch — called
across the cafeteria.

"Hey, foster freak! Break anything yet? Bet your 'new mommy' loves that."

Heat rushed through Jaden's chest. His hands curled into fists. He could see
himself lunging across the table, see the boy's shocked face, hear the shouts.

But instead, he stood up.

And walked out.

He didn't stop walking until he was home.

Mrs. Ortega was at the kitchen table when he burst through the door, out of
breath, his face hot.

"You're home early," she said, surprised.

He didn't answer. Just dropped his backpack and headed straight upstairs to the quiet room.

She followed a minute later, sitting on the floor outside.

After a long silence, she said softly, "That was brave, Jaden."

This time, when the tears came, they didn't feel like weakness.

They felt like… relief.

Part 3: Healing

Chapter 7: The Breakthrough

It happened on a rainy Saturday afternoon.

The kind of rain that turned the whole world silver, rattled against the windows, and sent thin streams down the glass. The sky outside was heavy and grey, and the house seemed quieter than usual, as though everyone inside was waiting for something to break.

Jaden was curled up in the quiet room, knees pulled to his chest, his hood drawn up over his head. The fairy lights blinked softly on the wall. He watched them without really seeing them, his mind replaying memories he hated—memories that clung to him like thorns.

There was a soft knock.

"Jaden?"

He didn't answer.

The door opened anyway, and Mrs. Ortega stepped inside, carrying two steaming mugs of hot chocolate. She sat cross-legged on the beanbag across from him, the smell of chocolate filling the room.

She didn't push.

She just set one of the mugs near his feet and started sipping from hers, watching the rain slide down the window.

At first, he stayed quiet.

Then, out of nowhere, he whispered, "Why do you even care?"

Her eyes met his.

"Because you matter," she said simply.

Something inside him cracked.

And before he could stop himself, the words came tumbling out — fast at first, then spilling like a river that had been dammed too long.

He told her about his mum — how she'd disappear for days, leaving him alone with nothing but cereal and fear. How she'd come back furious and drunk, smashing things, screaming at him for nothing. How he learned to hide in the closet when she was like that. And how, one night, she just… didn't come back.

He told her about the police. About being packed into a stranger's car in the middle of the night. About foster home after foster home, each one colder than the last. About how everyone always told him to "be good," but nobody ever asked what it was like to feel invisible.

When the words finally stopped, his voice was hoarse, his hands trembling.

Mrs. Ortega's eyes glistened. But she didn't look sad. She just nodded, her voice soft.

"Thank you," she said. "For trusting me enough to tell me."

And in that moment, for the first time, Jaden felt… lighter. Like maybe someone really did see him.

After that day, everything felt... different.

It wasn't that life magically got better overnight. He still got mad. Still had bad days. Still felt lost sometimes.

But the wall around his heart didn't feel quite so thick anymore.

Some nights he found himself in the quiet room just because — sitting on the beanbag, staring at the fairy lights, letting the quiet settle into his bones.

Other times he stayed downstairs, surprising himself.

One rainy evening, he sat next to Luis on the couch, watching him play video games. Luis handed him a controller without a word. They played three whole rounds in silence, and when Jaden won the third, Luis just smirked and muttered, "Beginner's luck."

One Saturday morning, Gabby sat on the rug in the living room, her hands full of bright hair elastics.

"Can I braid your hair?" she asked.

He groaned. "Why?"

"Because it's fun."

He let her do it.

When she finished, she burst into giggles, and he couldn't help but grin — even though his head was covered in crooked little braids.

Another night, Mrs. Ortega handed him a knife and a cutting board while she cooked dinner.

"You're on vegetable duty," she said, her eyes twinkling.

He rolled his eyes but started chopping anyway.

And when he thought she wasn't looking, he snuck a bite of carrot.

"I saw that," she said, laughing.

One warm evening, Mr. Ortega came home carrying a basketball.

"Wanna shoot some hoops?" he asked, holding it out.

Jaden hesitated.

Then nodded.

They played in the driveway until the sun dipped below the rooftops, both of them sweaty and breathless.

That night, lying in bed, he stared at the ceiling and thought:

Maybe this is what safe feels like.

Chapter 9: The Key

On his fifteenth birthday, Jaden woke up to the smell of pancakes and the sound of laughter downstairs.

When he walked into the kitchen, Gabby jumped up and shouted, "Happy birthday!" A crooked banner stretched across the wall, with glitter that rained down every time it shifted.

Luis gave him an awkward high-five before mumbling, "Don't get used to it."

After dinner, the whole family gathered around the table. Mrs. Ortega slid a small, square box toward him.

He frowned. "…What's this?"

"Open it," she said, smiling.

Inside was a silver key on a simple chain.

He stared at it, confused.

Mrs. Ortega's smile softened.

"It's the key to the quiet room," she explained. "It's yours now. You don't have to ask. You don't need permission. That room belongs to you just as much as it does to anyone in this house."

Jaden held the key in his palm, feeling its weight.

Something swelled in his chest — something warm and strange and almost too big to hold.

He slipped the chain over his head and clutched the key in his fist. "…Thanks," he whispered, his voice rough.

Mrs. Ortega reached across the table and squeezed his hand.

"You're family now, Jaden," she said. "And you always have a place here. No matter what."

Epilogue: Somewhere Safe

Months later, Jaden stood alone in the quiet room, the fairy lights glowing softly above him.

Life wasn't perfect.

There were still days when anger bubbled up in his chest. Still nights when he missed his mum so much it hurt to breathe.

But he wasn't alone anymore.

He had a place where he could sit and just... be.

He had people who didn't give up on him, even when he made it hard.

He touched the key around his neck, feeling its smooth edges, and smiled faintly.

He had a key.

And a home.

Somewhere safe.

And for the first time in his life...

That was enough.

Somewhere Safe by Emily Drage

Copyright © 2025 Emily Drage

This is a work of fiction. Names, characters, places, and incidents are either products of the author's imagination or used fictitiously. Any resemblance to actual events, locales, or persons, living or dead, is entirely coincidental

www.ingramcontent.com/pod-product-compliance
Lightning Source LLC
Chambersburg PA
CBHW070051100426
42734CB00040B/2982